New Year's Day

New Year's Day

New Year's Day

New Year's Day

New Year's Resolutions

New Year's Resolutions

Happy New Year

Happy New Year

Happy New Year

Happy New Year

Happy New Year

Happy New Year

Epiphany

Epiphany

Epiphany

Epiphany

The Epiphany of Our Lord

The Epiphany of Our Lord

The Epiphany of Our Lord

Lest we forget...
Martin Luther King, Jr.

Lest we forget...
Martin Luther King, Jr.

Lest we forget...
Martin Luther King, Jr.

Martin Luther King, Jr. Day

Martin Luther King, Jr. Day

Presidents' Day

Presidents' Day

Presidents' Day

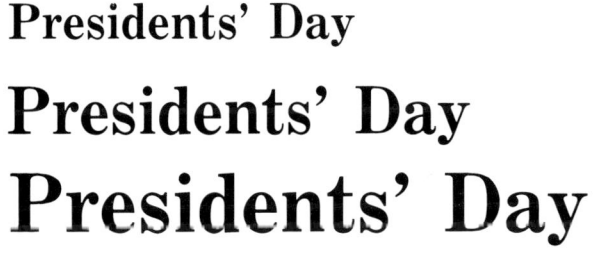

Lincoln's Birthday

Lincoln's Birthday

Lincoln's Birthday

Washington's Birthday

Washington's Birthday

Washington's Birthday

Lenten Season

Lenten Season

Lenten Season

Ash Wednesday

Ash Wednesday

Ash Wednesday

Ash Wednesday Service

Ash Wednesday Service

Ash Wednesday Service

Be Mine   Be Mine   Be Mine

Happy Valentine's Day

Happy Valentine's Day

Happy Valentine's Day

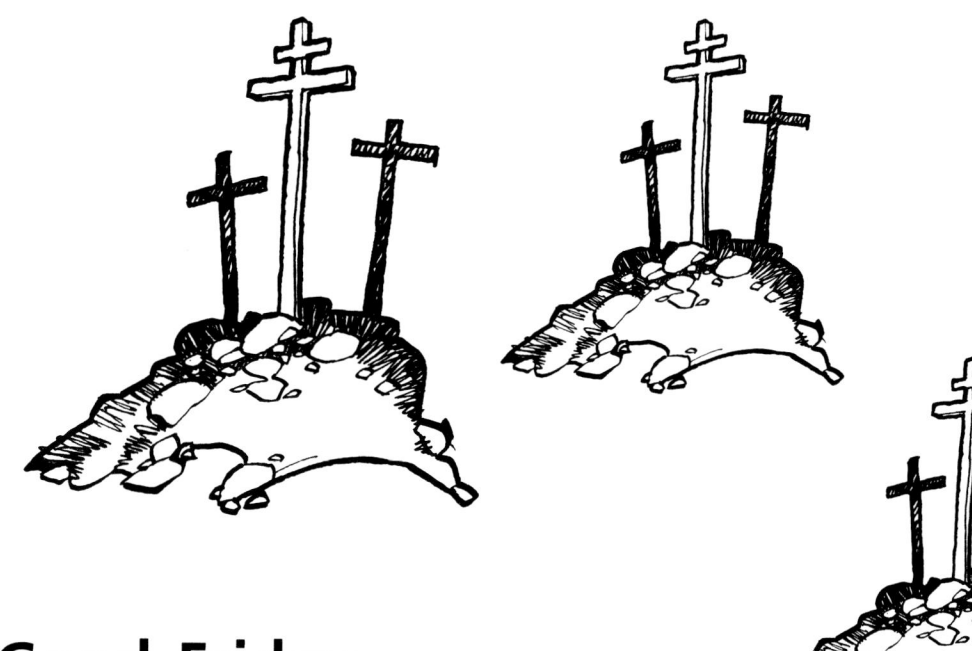

Good Friday

Good Friday

Palm Sunday

Palm Sunday

Holy Thursday

Holy Thursday

Holy Week Services

Holy Week Services

Passion/Palm Sunday

Passion/Palm Sunday

Columbus Day

Columbus Day

Columbus Day

Flag Day

Heritage Sunday

Flag Day

Heritage Sunday

Flag Day

Heritage Sunday

Brotherhood Sunday

Brotherhood Sunday

Brotherhood Sunday

Brotherhood Week

Brotherhood Week

Brotherhood Week

O Come, O Come, Emmanuel

O Come, O Come, Emmanuel

O Come, O Come, Emmanuel

Columbus Day

Columbus Day

Columbus Day

Flag Day

Heritage Sunday

Flag Day

Heritage Sunday

Flag Day

Heritage Sunday

Brotherhood Sunday

Brotherhood Sunday

Brotherhood Sunday

Brotherhood Week

Brotherhood Week

Brotherhood Week

O Come, O Come, Emmanuel

O Come, O Come, Emmanuel

O Come, O Come, Emmanuel

Festival of the Christian Home

Festival of the Christian Home

Festival of the Christian Home

Festival of the Christian Home

Festival of the Christian Home

Festival of the Christian Home

All Saints Day

All Saints Day

Labor Sunday

Labor Sunday

Labor Sunday

Labor Sunday

Labor Sunday

World Communion Day

World Communion Day

World Communion Day

World Communion Day

Bible Sunday

Bible Sunday

Bible Sunday

Laity Sunday

Laity Sunday

Laity Sunday

Veterans Day

Veterans Day

Veterans Day

Bible Sunday

Bible Sunday

Bible Sunday

Veterans Day

Veterans Day

Veterans Day

Laity Sunday

Laity Sunday

Laity Sunday

Stewardship Day

Stewardship Day

Stewardship Day

Labor Day

Labor Day

Labor Day

Stewardship Day

Stewardship Day

Stewardship Day

Labor Day

Labor Day

Labor Day

Holy Thursday Communion

Palm Sunday

Tenebrae

Tenebrae

Tenebrae

Palm Sunday

Palm Sunday

Holy Thursday Communion

Holy Thursday Communion

Easter Egg Hunt

Easter Egg Hunt

Easter Egg Hunt

He Is Risen!

He Is Risen!

He Is Risen!

Easter

Easter

Easter Music

Easter Music

Sunrise Service

Sunrise Service

Easter Sunrise Service

Easter Sunrise Service

Easter Lilies

Easter Lilies

Easter Lilies

Rural Life Sunday

Rural Life Sunday

Rural Life Sunday

Mother's Day

Mother's Day

Mother's Day

Mother's Day

Mother's Day

Mother's Day

Thanks Mothers

Thanks Mothers

May Fellowship Day

May Fellowship Day

May Fellowship Day

May Fellowship Day

Pentecost

Pentecost

Pentecost

Pentecost

Pentecost

Pentecost

Pentecost

Memorial Day

Memorial Day

Memorial Day

Memorial Day

Memorial Day

Memorial Day

Pentecost

Pentecost

Trinity Sunday

Trinity Sunday

Trinity Sunday

Trinity Sunday

Trinity Sunday

Trinity Sunday

The Ascension

The Ascension

The Ascension

Ascension

Ascension

Ascension

Transfiguration

Transfiguration

Transfiguration

Transfiguration of Our Lord

Transfiguration of Our Lord

Father's Day

Father's Day

Father's Day

Independence Sunday

Independence Sunday

Independence Sunday

I Love You, Dad!

I Love You, Dad!

I Love You, Dad!

Independence Day

Independence Day

Come, Ye Thankful People

Come, Ye Thankful People

Come, Ye Thankful People

Thanksgiving

Thanksgiving

Thanksgiving

We Are Thankful

We Are Thankful

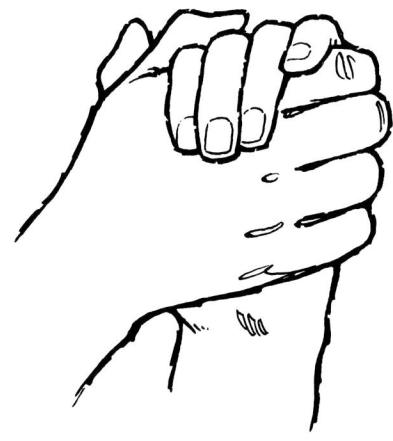 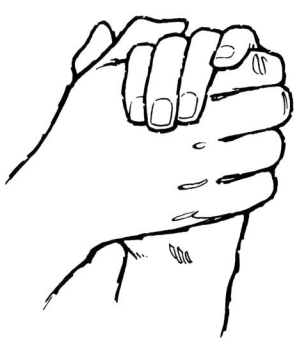 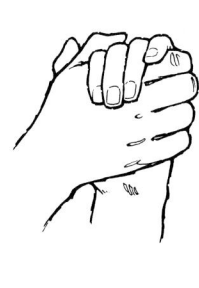

Thanksgiving

Thanksgiving

Thanksgiving

Thanksgiving

Thanksgiving

Thanksgiving

Thanksgiving Sunday

Thanksgiving Sunday

Thanksgiving Sunday

Let Us Give Thanks

Let Us Give Thanks

Let Us Give Thanks

𝕽𝖊𝖋𝖔𝖗𝖒𝖆𝖙𝖎𝖔𝖓 𝕯𝖆𝖞

𝕽𝖊𝖋𝖔𝖗𝖒𝖆𝖙𝖎𝖔𝖓 𝕯𝖆𝖞

𝕽𝖊𝖋𝖔𝖗𝖒𝖆𝖙𝖎𝖔𝖓 𝕯𝖆𝖞

𝕽𝖊𝖋𝖔𝖗𝖒𝖆𝖙𝖎𝖔𝖓 𝕯𝖆𝖞

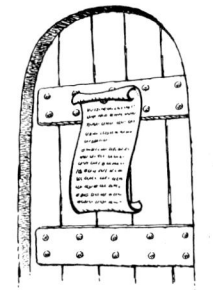

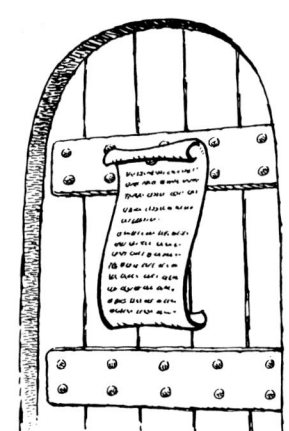

Reformation Day

Reformation Day

Reformation Day

Reformation Day

Reformation Day

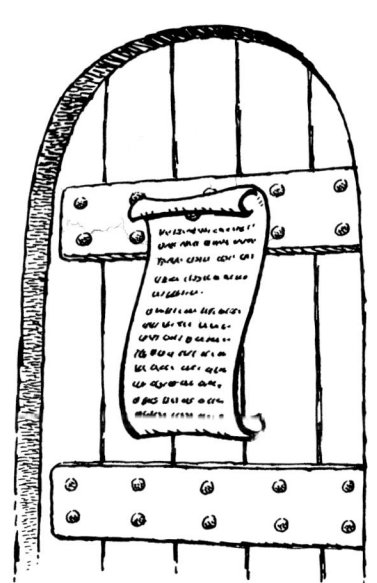

Reformation Day

A Mighty Fortress Is Our God

A Mighty Fortress Is Our God

A Mighty Fortress Is Our God

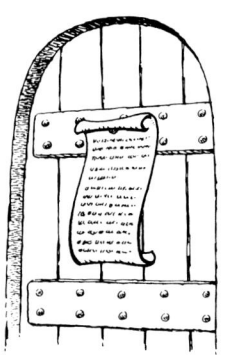

Advent

Advent

Advent

1st Sunday of Advent

2nd Sunday of Advent

3rd Sunday of Advent

4th Sunday of Advent

1st Sunday of Advent

2nd Sunday of Advent

3rd Sunday of Advent

4th Sunday of Advent

Christmas Eve

Christmas Eve

Midnight Mass

Midnight Mass

Midnight Mass

Christmas Season

Christmas Season

Christmas Season

Christmas Music

Christmas Music

Christmas Music

Christmas

Christmas

Christmas

JOY TO THE WORLD

JOY TO THE WORLD

Advent Schedule

Advent Schedule

Advent Schedule

Christmas Schedule

Christmas Schedule

Christmas Schedule

Christmas Joy

O Little Town of Bethlehem

Christmas Joy

O Little Town of Bethlehem

Christmas Joy

O Little Town of Bethlehem

Christmas Eve Communion

Christmas Eve Communion

Christmas Eve Communion

Christmas Calendar

Christmas Calendar

Christmas Calendar

Jazz up your holiday newsletters bulletins!

Looking for an inexpensive way to give holiday publications pizzazz? Try *The Great Clip Art Book for Holidays*. It offers you dozens of illustrations, words, and phrases that can be cut out and attached to newsletters, bulletins, church supper menus, and place cards.

Every piece of clip art is easy to use—and reuse! And clip art helps you convey each and every message with more impact.

The illustrations and phrases in this handy booklet are printed in various sizes—just pick the size that's appropriate for you! You will discover that *The Great Clip Art Book* is an ideal way to liven up your holiday publications!

Clip Art Books Available from Abingdon Press:

The Great Clip Art Book for Youth
The Great Clip Book for All Occasions
The Great Clip Art Book of Music
The Great Clip Art Book for Black Churches
The Great Multi-Ethnic Clip Art Book
The Great Clip Art Book of Bulletin Covers
The Great Clip Art Book of Favorite Bible Verses
The Great Clip Art Collection

Copyright © 1987 by Abingdon Press

Abingdon Press hereby grants permission to local churches and organizations to use the materials in this book without permission from the publisher if 1,000 or fewer copies are made. No further reproduction or distribution of this material is allowed without the written consent of Abingdon Press, 201 Eighth Avenue South, Nashville, Tennessee 37203.

Manufactured in the U.S.A.

Abingdon Press

ISBN 0-687-15716-1

Watch Night

Watch Night

Watch Night

New Year's Eve

New Year's Eve

New Year's Eve

Watch Night

Watch Night

Watch Night

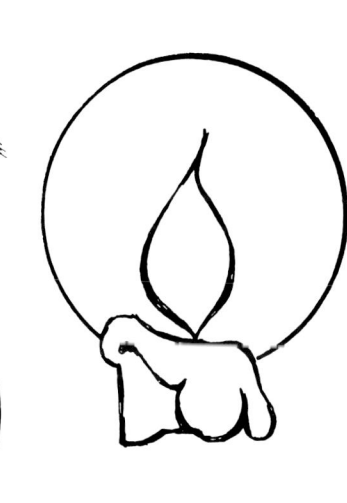

*Week of Prayer
for Christian Unity*

*Week of Prayer
for Christian Unity*

*Week of Prayer
for Christian Unity*

Mother's Day

All Saints Day

Thanksgiving

May Fellowship Day

Easter

INDEPENDENCE DAY

Passion/Palm Sunday

Transfiguration of Our Lord

Thanksgiving Sunday

A Mighty Fortress Is Our God